All About Animals

Cats

By Christina Wilsdon

Reader's Digest Young Families

Contents

Chapter 1
A Cat Story 5

Chapter 2
The Body of a Cat 13

Chapter 3
What Cats Do 21

Chapter 4
Kinds of Cats 29

Chapter 5
Cats in the World 37

Glossary
Wild Words 42

Index 44

Credits 45

Chapter 1
A Cat Story

Cat Words

A female cat is called a queen. A male cat is called a tom. Baby cats are called kittens. A female cat can have one to nine kittens in a litter. The usual number is between three and five kittens.

Mama Cat slipped into a closet. She climbed into a box tucked in a corner. A soft blanket lay inside the box. She pushed at the blanket with her paws until she had made a cozy nest. Mama Cat knew the box was a safe place. It had been set up for her by her owners. It was the perfect spot for giving birth to her babies.

Just a few hours later, five tiny kittens shared the box with Mama Cat. She licked the kittens from head to toe. They squirmed and squeaked.

Baby Cat felt Mama Cat's rough tongue on his fur. But he could not see her. His eyes were shut tight. His ears were folded against his head, so he could not hear her, either. All he could do was smell her.

Baby Cat was born with the urge to find his way to Mama Cat's belly. He wriggled closer and nuzzled her. Soon he was drinking her milk. He barely noticed his brothers and sisters as they tumbled over him to reach Mama Cat's belly too.

His tiny paws pressed against Mama Cat's body. He pushed them in and out of her soft fur. This helped make Mama Cat's milk flow.

As the kittens nursed, Mama Cat purred. She was tired but happy. Baby Cat and his littermates were tired now, too. They huddled together in a heap to keep warm, and Mama Cat snuggled up against them.

Each day Baby Cat's eyes opened a little bit more. By the time he was eight days old, Baby Cat was taking his first good looks at the world. He peered at his brothers and sisters. They had their eyes open, too, and they peered right back at him.

Another week passed. Now Baby Cat was ready to creep away from Mama Cat. He managed to get to the side of the box and started to find his way over and out! Mama Cat quickly grabbed him by the scruff of his neck and gently pulled him back in.

Baby Cat was still tiny, but he now weighed about nine ounces—three times as much as when he was born. His only food was Mama Cat's milk. He drank the milk from the same spot on Mama Cat's belly every day. If one of his brothers or sisters took his spot, he shoved and squirmed until he got it back.

By the time he was three weeks old, Baby Cat was and out of the box for most of the day. He tottered about the room with the other kittens. Mama Cat always kept an eye on them. She ran to any kitten that squealed in alarm.

Baby Blues

A kitten's eyes are always blue at birth. By the time it is about 12 weeks old, its eyes start changing to the color they will be for the rest of its life.

Time to Go

A kitten is ready to leave its mother and go to a new home when it is about 10 weeks old.

Baby Cat explored all kinds of new sights, smells, and sounds. One day, he discovered a new taste! He poked his nose into Mama Cat's food bowl. He licked the fishy food inside it. Then he licked his lips. But he didn't try it again. For now, he would stick to Mama Cat's milk.

When Baby Cat was about six weeks old, he was zipping all around the house with his brothers and sisters. When he grabbed hold of another kitten, the two of them would roll around like a fuzzy ball.

The kittens got into all kinds of mischief. They pulled yarn out of a knitting basket. They swatted small toys with their paws and lost them underneath the sofa.

One day the kittens knocked over a houseplant. It landed with a crash, and dirt flew everywhere. That was frightening! But their owner simply cleaned it up. Then she cuddled the kittens one by one. Baby Cat and the other kittens trusted the people in the house. Being handled gently by people would help them be good pets when they grew up.

Mama Cat kept a careful watch over her busy kittens. But she knew they would not hurt each other. The chasing, tackling, and tumbling was just play. It was also good exercise for the kittens' growing muscles.

Baby Cat learned a lot during his first few weeks of life. He learned to groom his own fur and how to use a litter box. He also decided that cat food tasted great!

Baby Cat will stop drinking Mama Cat's milk when he is about two months old. He will eat cat food after that. He will be all grown up when he is about a year old.

Chapter 2
The Body of a Cat

The feline family includes all cats, big and small—from huge Siberian tigers to the tiniest house cat.

Cat Cousins

House cats and lions belong to the same group of animals called the feline family. Like all felines, the house cat is a carnivore (pronounced *CAR nih vor*), which means it is a meat-eater. The way the body of a house cat is built helps it to hunt.

The bones in a house cat's back are connected less tightly to one another than those of other animals. This makes a cat's backbone very flexible. A house cat can easily move its body to climb, jump, and run. If you have ever watched a cat twist and turn while washing itself, you've seen how flexible it is.

Go, Cat, Go

A cat walks by moving both legs on one side of its body. Then it moves the legs on the other side. Camels and giraffes are the only other animals to move this way. A cat places its feet so carefully that its paw prints nearly form a straight line, as if it were walking on a tightrope.

To move faster, the cat trots like a horse. A running cat bounds on its two hind legs, then lands first on one front paw, then the other. A cat easily jumps up to high perches and walks on narrow ledges. It climbs up a tree headfirst and comes down the trunk backward, clinging with its claws. If it falls, a cat twists its head and then its body so that it lands safely on its feet.

Eyes

A cat's eyes sit at the front of its head, like yours do. This gives it the kind of vision it needs to judge how far away things are—a skill it needs to pounce on a mouse.

A cat can see six times better than you can in dim light. The dark pupil in the middle of a cat's eye opens into a wide, round circle to let in as much light as possible. Light also bounces off the inside back of each eye. This gives the cat a second chance to use some of the light to help it see. It also makes a cat's eyes glow in the dark when you shine a flashlight at it!

Whiskers

Sprouting from either side of a cat's face are long, stiff hairs called whiskers. A typical cat has about 24 whiskers. It also has whiskery hairs above its eyes, around its face, and on its legs too.

A cat's whiskers are sensitive to touch. They are connected to the brain by many nerves and can detect even the slightest motion of air. This helps a cat feel its way around in dim light or darkness.

A cat can move the whiskers on its snout forward and back. This is useful because a cat's close-up vision is poor. Feeling with its whiskers helps the cat find things that it can't see but are "right under its nose."

Super Hearing

A cat can hear very high-pitched sounds, like the squeaking of mice. It moves its ears in all directions to listen for sounds. Many pet cats will run to the door long before a visitor even gets there!

A cat's eyes are so beautiful that some glowing gems are known as "cat's eyes." Orange, gold, yellow, green, and blue are among the colors a cat's eyes can be.

Sharp Tongue

Have you ever been licked by a friendly cat? Then you know that a cat's tongue feels rough. It is covered with rough bumps. The bumps let a cat lick small bits of meat off a bone. The roughness also helps a cat groom its fur.

A cat usually has five toes on each front paw and four toes on each hind paw. Sometimes cats are born with extra toes.

Teeth...

A grown-up cat has 30 teeth. The biggest teeth are the four long, sharp fangs called canines. These teeth are used to grab and kill prey. They also help tear apart meat.

In between the top and bottom canines are twelve little teeth called incisors. A cat uses these to nibble food and to groom its fur.

Behind the fangs are sharp teeth called carnassials (pronounced *car NAS ee uls*). These pointy teeth work like scissors to shred meat. A cat turns its head sideways to slice cut food with its carnassials. It does not chew and grind food with its hind teeth as you do.

...And Claws!

Each cat toe has a sharp claw. A cat uses its claws to hold prey, to climb, and to protect itself by scratching at an attacker. They are kept hidden inside the cat's paws. This helps keep the claws sharp. Claws that stick out would be worn down by scraping against the ground.

A cat's claws pop out when a cat attacks prey or defends itself. This happens automatically as the cat tightens muscles in its legs. The cat's toes spread apart at the same time. You can see this when a cat stretches after a nap.

Chapter 3
What Cats Do

You can see hunting behavior just by watching a cat at play. It will stalk and pounce upon a blade of grass or a wiggling string. A cat will chase toys that you throw. Some cats will even chase the beam of a flashlight!

Surprise Attacks

A domestic cat hunts the same way that wild cats do. It sneaks up quietly on its prey. This is called stalking. A stalking cat crouches down and slinks along nearly on its belly. If it thinks it has been spotted by its prey, it stands as still as a statue until its prey relaxes. When the cat is close to its prey, it charges. It may catch its prey in just one bound or chase it for a short distance.

Cats play with other cats if they know them well. Kittens stalk and pounce on each other as well as their mother's tail. They play-fight until they are exhausted. Grown-up cats play less. But they will also stalk a friend and wrestle or play with their owner. Some cats like to launch surprise attacks on people's ankles as they walk by!

Claw Care

Claws become dull with use. Cats use their teeth to pull off the outer layer of each claw to uncover a new, sharp layer underneath.

Many people think a cat is sharpening its claws when it hooks them into a tree and scratches. Actually, the cat does this to stretch its muscles. But the action also helps to remove the claws' old outer layers. Clawing is also a way for the cat to leave its scent on the tree for other cats to smell.

Keeping Clean

A cat may spend half of its waking hours grooming itself. It licks its fur with its raspy tongue, which works like a comb to remove dirt. Licking also spreads oils made in the cat's skin across its fur. These oils give a cat's fur its shine. They also contain scents that the cat uses to mark its territory by rubbing against objects.

A cat's body is so flexible that it can reach almost every part of its body as it grooms. It can even twist its neck to lick its own shoulders! A cat uses its teeth to pull snarls out of its fur and dirt out of its paws.

Cats also groom each other. A female cat licks her kittens from the moment they are born. Kittens start grooming themselves when they are about four weeks old. Cats that live together and are friends also lick each other. Some cats even "groom" their owners by licking them!

Cat Naps

A cat may rest up to 14 hours a day. An old cat or a cat living in a hot climate may rest more! This rest is made up of long, deep sleeps and many short naps.

To wash its face, a cat first licks its front paws. Then it rubs the wet paw over its ears and on its face.

Sniff!
Cats mark their territory by rubbing their scent onto objects. A cat does this by rubbing its chin, the sides of its face, or even its whole body against different things—such as a tree, a chair, or your leg!

This cat's meow may mean "let me in," "look at me," or "where's the cat food?"

Cat Talk

A cat meows to get attention. It purrs when it is content and feels safe. Female cats purr to their kittens, and kittens purr as they nurse. Many cats purr when they are stroked. Oddly, a nervous cat may also purr.

Cats use other sounds when they are upset. An angry cat growls and hisses. A fearful cat hisses, too. A very angry cat can make a noise that sounds like a scream.

Body Language

A cat's ears, whiskers, and tail can show how a cat is feeling. A curious, friendly cat pricks up its ears, holds its tail up straight, and points its whiskers forward. A fearful cat folds back its ears and whiskers. An annoyed cat lashes its tail.

A cat often uses its whole body to express itself. It may welcome its owner or a feline friend by rolling over and showing its belly. But an aggressive cat approaches another cat with ears folded back, back arched, and fur puffed up to make it look bigger. A fearful cat holds its ears out sideways. It may arch its back and puff up its fur, or it may crouch to defend itself.

Cats often begin a fight by staring at each other. A scared cat's pupils grow round and large. A contented cat may close its eyes halfway.

Chapter 4
Kinds of Cats

Cat Breeds

A cat that belongs to a special breed has a certain kind of fur, shape, or color that it shares with other cats of the same breed. Cat breeds are divided into two main groups: short-haired breeds and long-haired breeds.

Short-Haired Cats

Short-haired breeds are usually divided into two groups. One group is simply called shorthairs. The other group is called foreign, or Oriental, shorthairs. Foreign shorthairs have leaner bodies and thinner, wedge-shaped heads than other shorthairs.

The British shorthair is a typical shorthair. It is a round-faced, sturdy cat. Its cousin, the American shorthair, is descended from the cats that helped the early settlers control mice and rats on their farms.

The Siamese cat is one of the most popular foreign shorthairs. A Siamese has long, thin legs and a long, slim tail, which are darker than its body. The Siamese's face and ears are darker, too. Siamese cats are famous for yowling and "talking" a lot.

Other foreign shorthairs include the Korat, with its thick fur of bluish silver, and the all-black Bombay.

Long-Haired Cats

The first long-haired cats, which came from parts of Asia, were brought to Europe about 500 years ago. People were used to short-haired cats, so cats with extra-long hair were new and unusual. Over time, these cats were bred to produce new long-haired breeds.

One of these long-haired breeds is the Angora. It is named after a place in the country of Turkey, where its ancestors came from. Its fur is long, silky, and fluffy. In summer, it sheds lots of hair to keep cool. The first Angoras were all white, but modern Angoras come in many colors.

Good Looks Take Work

All long-haired cats need to be brushed to keep their fur clean. Brushing also keeps the fur free of tangled clumps, called mats.

Another long-haired breed is the Persian. The first Persian cats came from Iran, which was once called Persia. A Persian cat has long outer fur that may be nearly five inches long! Under this long hair is a fuzzy undercoat. This thick, long fur makes a Persian look plump.

Other long-haired breeds include Birmans, Turkish Vans, and Maine Coon cats.

Just Cats!

Most pet cats are a mixture of breeds. A veterinarian may call a cat like this a domestic shorthair, a domestic longhair, or a "mixed breed." Most people simply call them house cats, kitties, or moggies!

Persian cats, like this one, have flatter faces and shorter noses than Angoras.

Chocolate Cats?

Cat breeders use different words to describe cats' colors. A dark-gray cat is said to be blue. A pale-gray cat is lilac or lavender. A tan cat is called cream. An orange cat is called a red cat. A brown cat may be called chocolate, while a reddish brown one is called cinnamon.

A calico is not a breed of cat—it is the color pattern of the cat's coat. Domestic shorthairs, Persians, and Manx are just a few of the breeds that can sport the colors of a calico.

Colorful Kitties

Cats' coats come in a wide variety of colors and patterns. A cat can be all one color—black, white, red, or gray. This is called solid, or self, coloring. A cat whose coat has two solid colors is called a bicolor.

Many bicolors are splashed with large patches of color and white. But one bicolor looks as if it is wearing a formal black-and-white suit! This bicolor is the tuxedo cat. A tuxedo cat has a black body and tail, white paws, and a white belly. It often has white on its face, too.

Tricolor cats, such as the tortoiseshell, have three colors. Tortoiseshell is a combination of red, cream, and black hairs mixed together. A tortoiseshell cat is often called a tortie. If it has striped markings mixed in, it is called a torbie. One of the most dazzling patterns is called tortie-and-white, or calico. A calico cat has big patches of black, red, and cream or white.

Stripes, Spots, and Points

Striped cats are called tabby cats. Tabby markings can also include rows of spots. The tabby pattern is the oldest and most basic cat color. Many wild species of cats are also striped or spotted.

Cats with pale bodies and dark legs, faces, ears, and tails are called colorpoint cats. Siamese cats are one kind of colorpoint cat. They are born pale all over. The darker points develop as they grow.

Chapter 5
Cats in the World

Unlucky Cats!
Some people still hold beliefs about cats and luck. Some think a black cat is bad luck. But not in England! There, a black cat is good luck—but a white cat brings bad luck if you see it on the way to school!

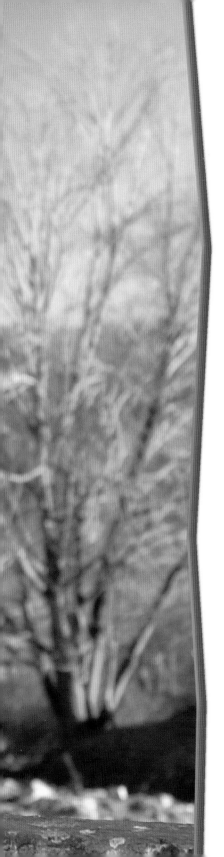

Cats and People

The ancestor of the domestic cat is thought to be the African wildcat. This wild species lives in parts of Africa and the Middle East. It looks a bit like a big, heavy, pale orange tabby cat. It preys on small animals, such as insects, rodents, and birds.

Nobody knows just where or when the first wildcat was tamed. But people have kept cats as pets and mousers for nearly 5,000 years. Over time, cats have changed little by little as they adapted to living with humans.

In ancient Egypt, cats earned respect by getting rid of mice and rats that lived in grain bins. The ancient Egyptians even worshipped cats. They believed a cat was the sacred pet of an Egyptian goddess. After cats died, they were wrapped in linen and made into mummies.

Good Luck, Bad Luck

For the past 2,000 years, cats and humans have shared an up-and-down history.

Sometimes people treated cats very well. People in parts of France believed some cats were magic. If the cats were treated nicely, they brought good luck. In China, people respected the cat's mouse-hunting skills and thought cats could chase away evil spirits.

At other times, people thought cats might be devils or witches. Many cats were killed in Europe starting in the 1400s because people believed they were evil spirits.

The Future of Cats

Cats are very popular as pets. In the United States alone, there are nearly 78 million pet cats. Pet cats have outnumbered dogs since 1996.

One problem is that when pet cats roam outdoors, they sometimes kill large numbers of birds and other small animals. On some islands, cats have caused certain kinds of birds to become rare or even extinct. Pet owners are often encouraged to keep their cats indoors.

Another problem is cat overpopulation. There are too many cats and not enough homes for them all. Millions of cats are brought into animal shelters each year. Luckily, many people help prevent cat overpopulation by spaying or neutering their cats. These operations stop cats from having kittens. This gives cats who are already living in shelters a better chance at finding a new home—where they can become somebody's "purr-fect" pet.

Fast Facts About House Cats

Scientific name	*Felis catus*
Class	Mammalia
Order	Carnivora
Size	Up to 10 inches tall at the shoulder
Weight	Up to 20 pounds
Life span	Usually up to 20 years

Glossary of Wild Words

bicolor — a cat that has a coat of two solid colors

blue — a word for any dark-gray cat

breed — a specific kind of cat

carnassials — teeth used for slicing meat

claws — a cat's sharp nails

colorpoint — a cat with legs, ears, tail, and face darker than the body

habitat — the natural environment where an animal or plant lives

kitten — a baby cat

litter — a group of kittens born at the same time

litter box — a box containing gravel or other materials that a cat uses as a bathroom

long-haired — a category of cat breeds that have long hair

moggies	another word for house cats
predator	an animal that hunts and eats other animals to survive
prey	animals that are hunted by other animals for food
purr	a rumbling sound often made by a contented cat
queen	a female cat
scratching post	a post covered with carpet or rope for a cat to claw
short-haired	a category of cat breeds that have short hair
species	a group of living things that are the same in many ways
territory	an area of land that an animal marks as its own
tom	a male cat
tortie	another word for a tortoiseshell cat

Index

A

Angora cats 32, 33

B

birth 7
bones 15
breeds 31-35

C

calico cats 34, 35
claws 19, 23
climbing 15, 19
colors 31, 32, 34-35
communication 26-27, 31

E

ears 7, 17, 27, 31
eating 7, 8, 18, 19
eye color 8, 17
eyes 7, 8, 16, 17, 27

F

feline family 14, 15, 39
female cats 6, 9
food 7, 8, 11
fur 24, 31-35

G

grooming 11, 18, 19, 24-25, 32
growth 8-11

H

hearing 17
humans 11, 38-40
hunting 22-23

J

jumping 15

K

kittens 6-11, 23, 24, 27, 30

L

licking 7, 8, 18, 25
life span 40
long-haired breeds 32-33

M

male cats 6
markings 34, 35
mixed breeds 32
mother cats 7, 8, 24, 27

P

paws 7, 15, 18, 19, 24, 25
Persian cats 32, 33

R

running 11, 15

S

scent marking 23, 24, 26
short-haired breeds 31
Siamese cats 31
sleeping 24
sounds 26, 27, 31
stalking 22, 23
stretching 23
superstitions 38-39

T

tail 27
teeth 19, 23, 24
territory 24, 26
toes 19
tongue 8, 24
tortoiseshell cats 35

W

walking 8, 15
whiskers 16, 27
wild cats 39